IMAGES
of America

FORT GORDON

Pictured are Mrs. B. M. Boykin (right) and her daughter Florence Boykin (left). For her work at the hostess house, Mrs. Boykin was known as the "Mother of Camp Gordon." (Courtesy of the U.S. Army Signal Corps Museum.)

ON THE COVER: Firearms practice and scoring was an important part of the introduction process to the military. In this image, soldiers at Camp Gordon in Atlanta, Georgia, are seen qualifying with their weapons. Notice the scorecards in their hats. (Courtesy of the U.S. Army Signal Corps Museum.)

IMAGES
of America

FORT GORDON

Sean Joiner, Gerald Smith, Ph.D,
and Robert Anzuoni

ARCADIA
PUBLISHING

Copyright © 2009 by Sean Joiner, Gerald Smith, Ph.D, and Robert Anzuoni
ISBN 978-0-7385-6812-6

Published by Arcadia Publishing
Charleston, South Carolina

Printed in the United States of America

Library of Congress Control Number: 2008941207

For all general information contact Arcadia Publishing at:
Telephone 843-853-2070
Fax 843-853-0044
E-mail sales@arcadiapublishing.com
For customer service and orders:
Toll-Free 1-888-313-2665

Visit us on the Internet at www.arcadiapublishing.com

Camp Gordon, presently the home of Fort Gordon, is dedicated to all the past, present, and future military personnel who have and will train there.

This book is dedicated to U.S. Army Pfc. Stephen P. Snowberger III, who died during combat operations in Baghdad, Iraq, on May 11, 2006. Thank you for serving our country.

Contents

Acknowledgments

The authors would like to acknowledge the men who are named in the images contained within this work. They are as follows: Richard Shanley, William Burns, George Swords, Joseph Edwards, Robert Junge, Stanley Okuniewski, Richard Koltz, Charles Miller, Richard Bartlett, Donald Smith, Thomas Schied, Angelo J. Ballaera, Clarence Souder, Hugh Thornton, Robert Ziegler, Donald Lobue, Donald Benson, George Packis, John Farrell, and Sam Feenstra. Even without knowing it, through the photographs on these pages, you have made this book possible.

All photographs that are not listed as being provided by the U.S. Army Signal Corps Museum are from the private collection of Sean Joiner.

Introduction

Originally established as Camp Gordon near Atlanta, Georgia, in 1917, Fort Gordon has served as an important training center for the U.S. Army during World War I, World War II, the Korean War, the Vietnam War, and the Gulf War. Today, as home of the U.S. Army Signal Center, the installation continues to train soldiers for the global war on terrorism.

Named for John Brown Gordon, a Confederate general, U.S. senator, and governor of Georgia, Camp Gordon was established near Atlanta in 1917 to train soldiers for World War I. The famed 82nd Division was formed and trained there for its service on the battlefields of France. It was while at Camp Gordon that the 82nd adopted its nickname, the All American, because it was a national army division made up of conscripts from throughout the United States. Although there were people from many different ethnic backgrounds, they were all Americans fighting for their country. Soon the division adopted the red, white, and blue shoulder sleeve insignia with the double "A" in the center to represent All American. Famous alumni include Sgt. Alvin York, whom Gen. John J. Pershing called the "greatest soldier of World War I;" Jonathan Wainwright, the division G-3 (operations officer) who earned the Medal of Honor in World War II; and Gordon Johnston, the division chief of staff who was a signal corps Medal of Honor recipient during the Philippine Insurrection.

With the end of World War I in November 1918, there was no longer a need for such a vast number of training camps. By 1919, the United States was demobilizing and closing camps such as Camp Gordon. By the 1920s, the land was sold off, and Atlanta grew. The Peachtree-DeKalb Airport soon occupied most of the former Camp Gordon. It would take another world war to revive the name of Camp Gordon.

Even before the attack on Pearl Harbor, the United States began to mobilize for the war that had started in Europe in 1939. Industry was gearing up to supply the Allied nations, and by 1941, troops were being mobilized once again. New training camps were needed to accommodate this new army.

In 1941, construction began on a camp near Augusta, Georgia. The post was dedicated on October 18, 1941, as Camp Gordon, once again in honor of John Brown Gordon. During World War II, various units conducted training at Camp Gordon, including the 4th Infantry Division (Ivy Division), the 26th Infantry Division (Yankee Division), and the 10th Armored Division (Tiger Division). The 4th Signal Company of the 4th Infantry Division included a Comanche code talker team that landed in Normandy on D-Day. All three divisions participated in the Battle of the Bulge.

After World War II, the United States realized it needed to remain prepared for the cold war. Camp Gordon was kept open, and the Signal Corps Training Center and Military Police School were located there in 1948. An Engineer Aviation Unit Training was activated in 1949 but was inactivated in 1950. On March 21, 1956, General Order No. 11 designated Camp Gordon as Fort Gordon, recognizing its permanent role as a key training installation. In 1964, ground was broken for a new Southeast Signal School complex. During the 1960s, Fort Gordon served as a Basic Combat and Advanced Individual Training facility for many soldiers deploying to Vietnam. The year 1965 saw the activation of an Officer Candidate School, which remained in operation until 1968.

In the 1970s, the U.S. Army underwent a realignment that resulted in moving several organizations and closing some installations. The Signal Center at Fort Monmouth, New Jersey, was relocated to Fort Gordon in 1974, while the Military Police School moved to Fort McClellan, Alabama.

Since 1974, Fort Gordon has been home to the U.S. Army Signal Corps. With the implementation of the U.S. Army Regimental System in 1986, Fort Gordon also became home of the Signal Regiment. Today the Signal Center at Fort Gordon is responsible for the training of all signal soldiers and the manning of signal units throughout the army. U.S. Navy and Air Force detachments also conduct training at Fort Gordon. The installation is also home to the 15th Signal Brigade, the 35th Signal Brigade, the 7th Signal Command, the 513th Military Intelligence Brigade, and the Eisenhower Army Medical Center.

—Robert Anzuoni

One

The Beginning

Camp Gordon, established near Atlanta, Georgia, in 1917, was named for John Brown Gordon, a Confederate general, U.S. senator, and governor of Georgia. Gordon served with distinction during the Civil War. His last official duty was to surrender Confederate general Robert E. Lee's troops at Appomattox. (Courtesy of the U.S. Army Signal Corps Museum.)

Here is the cover of a souvenir booklet for Camp Gordon in Atlanta, Georgia. Such booklets made it easy for soldiers to get photographs of places where they were stationed. The image on the cover shows Gen. John B. Gordon wearing a World War I–period uniform as he smiles upon soldiers in formation at Camp Gordon. (Courtesy of the U.S. Army Signal Corps Museum.)

This is the headquarters of the 82nd Division. The unit was known as the "All American" because it was composed of soldiers of many ethnic backgrounds from every state in the nation. The division participated in the Lorraine, St. Mihiel, and Meuse-Argonne campaigns in France during World War I. (Courtesy of the U.S. Army Signal Corps Museum.)

The Knights of Columbus Hall served as a recreational facility for all soldiers. The Knights of Columbus, founded in 1882, is an international Catholic men's organization dedicated to the principles of charity, unity, fraternity, and patriotism. (Courtesy of the U.S. Army Signal Corps Museum.)

Soldiers attend Mass in the Knights of Columbus Hall. The army made every attempt to provide for religious services for the soldiers. (Courtesy of the U.S. Army Signal Corps Museum.)

The YMCA (Young Men's Christian Association) building is shown in this photograph. The YMCA supported many activities for the morale of the soldiers. (Courtesy of the U.S. Army Signal Corps Museum.)

A review of the troops was a timely necessity. Military reviews have a long history. A review allows the commander to see his troops and provides the opportunity for soldiers to see their commander. A division review could be a big affair, since there were 28,000 soldiers in a division during World War I. (Courtesy of the U.S. Army Signal Corps Museum.)

Wagons passing in review are shown here. Most of the supplies of a World War I division were transported in such wagons. (Courtesy of the U.S. Army Signal Corps Museum.)

Company H, 327th Infantry Regiment, 164th Brigade, 82nd Division is shown here at Camp Gordon. (Courtesy of the U.S. Army Signal Corps Museum.)

Receiving a letter from home was always a special occasion. Getting mail could be a highlight to the otherwise boring routine of army life in a training camp. (Courtesy of the U.S. Army Signal Corps Museum.)

Stretcher bearers (above) and the band (below) of the 328th Infantry Regiment, 164th Brigade, 82nd Division are pictured here. Stretcher bearers played an important role in evacuating casualties to field hospitals. The band provided military music for ceremonies as well as entertainment for the soldiers. (Courtesy of the U.S. Army Signal Corps Museum.)

The Camp Gordon hospital nurses were angels in their own right. A key role for women during World War I was serving as nurses to aid in the war effort. (Courtesy of the U.S. Army Signal Corps Museum.)

Pictured here is training with the M-1917 rifle. Marksmanship is key to battlefield success for an infantryman. (Courtesy of the U.S. Army Signal Corps Museum.)

Training on a range with the Lewis machine gun was a tactical must for a soldier. Machine guns revolutionized warfare with their high volume of fire. The Lewis gun was a favorite light machine gun among many nations. (Courtesy of the U.S. Army Signal Corps Museum.)

This was the first kitchen established at Camp Gordon. An army cannot fight without food! (Courtesy of the U.S. Army Signal Corps Museum.)

Shown here is the guard mount at the 325th Infantry Regiment guard house. Pulling guard duty was a basic experience of army life. The 325th Infantry was part of the 163rd Brigade, 82nd Division. (Courtesy of the U.S. Army Signal Corps Museum.)

A gun crew of the B Battery, 320th Field Artillery Regiment, 157th Field Artillery Brigade practices on a firing range in April 1918. This U.S. piece would be exchanged for French 75-millimeter guns upon arrival in France to make resupply easier. (Courtesy of the U.S. Army Signal Corps Museum.)

Bayonet practice was crucial to a soldier's training. The use of bayonets in trench warfare was critical for survival as well as for the shock effect during an attack. (Courtesy of the U.S. Army Signal Corps Museum.)

The 320th Field Artillery at mess was a daily scene full of hungry soldiers. Soldiers were served hot meals in their mess kits and canteen cups. (Courtesy of the U.S. Army Signal Corps Museum.)

Cooks at the Camp Gordon hospital are shown in this image. (Courtesy of the U.S. Army Signal Corps Museum.)

Alvin C. York, G Company, 328th Infantry Regiment, 164th Brigade, 82nd Division was one of the greatest men of his generation. York trained at Camp Gordon. Though a conscientious objector, he decided to fight. York earned the Medal of Honor during fighting in the Argonne Forest on October 6, 1918. He is pictured at the scene of the battle after the war. York was the most highly decorated American soldier of World War I. (Courtesy of the U.S. Army Signal Corps Museum.)

Two

Around the Area

Soldiers often left Camp Gordon to pass the time when leave was available. Here a view of Broad Street in Augusta, Georgia, is seen from the corner of Eighth and Greene Streets. Signs representing Matheny Peebles and Seigler Realtors can be seen at 322 Broad Street. Also, in the distance other businesses such as the Central Finance Company, the City Shoe Repair, Jay Jewelers, and De Soto can be seen. Broad Street was an area where soldiers frequented cocktail lounges and businesses offering adult entertainment.

This photograph shows Broad Street at Sixth Street, with the photographer facing west. Notice the old-timey street lamp on the corner next to the 19th Hole.

Broad Street at Seventh Street shows Augusta's Confederate monument in the distance. Other landmarks that can be seen in the photograph are the Augusta Herald, the Miller Theatre, and the WRDW radio station.

Common tourist attractions in downtown Augusta consisted of Civil War–related sites. In this photograph, the Confederate monument on Broad Street is visible next to the Lamar Building. The soldier on top was modeled after a famous Civil War veteran named Benson Berry.

The Imperial Theatre sits behind the Confederate monument. The Imperial was an important anchor in downtown Augusta providing theater entertainment for servicemen. Just west of the Imperial is the Fred Astaire Studio, which gave instructions on ballet, tap, tango, samba, swing, and the mambo. Underneath the studio sits the Georgia Sporting Goods store, which became a one-stop spot for athletic soldiers.

Here a view of the Confederate monument is seen in front of the Augusta Herald building. To the right of the newspaper building sit Haverty's Furniture and the Georgia Railroad Bank. A legend tells of Benson Berry climbing down from the monument on nights when the moon is full. He is said to parade up and down Broad Street with his gun, honoring the sons of the South that fell in battle during the Civil War.

A soldier poses for a photograph at an unknown location in downtown Augusta. He is having fun with a playful position on a swing. Behind him, a sign advertises Krispy Crackers.

The Georgia Railroad was an important transportation hub for servicemen traveling into and out of Augusta, Georgia. The railway was chartered in 1833, along with a bank that eventually came onto the scene supporting Augusta residents and soldiers with financial services.

The Georgia Railroad became known as Georgia Railroad and Banking in 1936. The banking side was seen as more profitable.

Famous Augustan John Pendelton King was the president of the railroad from 1841 to 1878. Augusta has a park named after him. This date was set for rain. There were not many people out, but the soldier taking this picture captured the plaza in front of the railroad station.

An unidentified soldier stands next to a loved one in front of a passenger car.

The Augusta Regional Airport is a hub of activity because of its use as a military landing zone for aircraft as well as the transportation of military officers by commercial airlines. The airport was originally known as Bush Field when it was bought through a bond issue in 1948. Eventually, airlines such as Delta and Eastern became interested in the airport, at which time they set up flight operations. Notice the aircraft on the tarmac is an early Delta passenger airplane that was in operation when Bush Field first opened.

In the early days of the Bush Field Airport, terminals were small. Here is the outside of the terminal where soldiers would wait for their rides to post.

The First Baptist Church sits on the corner of Eighth and Greene Streets. It is here that the Southern Baptist Convention was established in 1845.

The Lanier Monument is located on Greene Street in Augusta.

Shown here is a beautiful example of Greek Revival architecture in downtown Augusta.

The Cyclorama at Grant Park is the world's largest three-dimensional picture. It features the Battle of Atlanta. The picture ranges 50 feet in height and 500 feet in circumference. The Cyclorama and other tourist sites in Atlanta were common overnight venues when a soldier had leave.

In this photograph, soldiers from Camp Gordon are preparing to venture inside the Cyclorama to learn about Civil War–era Atlanta.

On top of Stone Mountain, Joe Ballaera views the scene. The edifice is the largest body of exposed granite on earth. It stretches 7 miles in circumference and stands 800 feet above the surrounding terrain.

Bob Ziegler pops his head in front of the camera in this shot of Main Street in Atlanta on a Sunday morning before getting ready to head back to Fort Gordon.

Sgt. Roger Sterling clowns around and poses with a Confederate cap that was a souvenir from Stone Mountain Park.

The men and horses carved into Stone Mountain stand defiant. The soldiers had the opportunity to purchase field glasses, souvenirs, pennants, cards, and folders at the studio that is pictured in front of the grand granite mountain.

Joe Ballaera, Joe Lobue, and Bob Junge assemble behind an automobile for a group picture at Stone Mountain before leaving to come back to Camp Gordon.

In this historic postcard, a bird's-eye view of Camp Gordon shows the parade ground. A postmark on the back is dated October 21, 1951, Augusta, Georgia. The sender, Pvt. Robert T. Junge, writes to R. E. Junge in Madison, Wisconsin, the following. "Hi, Just a card to say 'hello' and send my love. A photo of our lovely camp . . . stays warm, but rained today on and off . . . Love Bob."

The post theater on Camp Gordon provided many hours of entertainment for military personnel. Robert T. Junge writes on November 30, 1951, "Just a card to let you know alls well. Got the box Tuesday in fine shape. The popcorn balls are really fine! That's the treat I enjoy most! They really hit the spot. Open one up anytime and eat it. Got paid today and that puts you closer to getting home! Love Bob."

The author of many postcards sent to his family from Camp Gordon, Robert T. Junge sent several showing Augusta landmarks. Shown here is the Bon Air Hotel. It is listed as one of the South's largest and finest hotels. It is noted for its delicious foods and the ultramodern Terrace Room, known for dinner and supper dancing. Augusta is considered by many as the golf center of America. Junge writes on December 5, 1951, "Hi, another picture of Augusta here. Fine day—windows and doors open—sun warm and bright. Rained hard yesterday, but dried off fine and sun was out for retreat. Late nite. Will try to phone this weekend. Love Bob."

The Oliver General Hospital at Camp Gordon is seen here in an almost untouched scene surrounded by a lush green landscape. Robert T. Junge writes on January 4, 1951, "Just a card this a.m. to say hi, and tell you a letter follows shortly. Got a registered letter from Aunt Maeta yesterday. Photo $3.00 and a card. She seems to be enjoying her stay in Florida. This is the Oliver General Hospital I refer to at times. Love Bob."

The Augusta City Hospital postcard lists the care-giving center as one of the greatest assets of the city, manned by efficient physicians and surgeons with a well-trained nursing staff and careful dietitians. Robert T. Junge writes on February 1, 1952, "Hi, here's your card, but not from Chi. or Atlanta. Had uneventful trip to Chi. but Chuck wanted to go downtown, so we spent all our time in the loop. Most interesting trip. Love Bob."

This postcard of the Municipal Auditorium states it was dedicated in April 1940 and is one of the largest, most usable, and modern auditoriums in the southeast. It is constructed of Augusta brick, steel, and concrete. The main auditorium has a music hall with a common stage and a combined seating capacity of 5,064, all with a view of the stage. If needed, arrangements could be made for an additional 1,000 seats.

The Southern Finance and Marion Building in Augusta, Georgia, is one of the city's first skyscrapers. Robert T. Junge writes on March 27, 1951, "Hi, Just a note. Had a strong workout today—ju-jitsu—as it is known in the Army—judo. Plenty tired tonight. Were getting a fast training for sure. Will get to drive sometime this week I think. Our next bivouac will consist mainly of night problems, blackout driving, etc. Will write you a letter soon, Love Bob."

The First Presbyterian Church in Augusta, Georgia, is listed as being organized in 1804. On the postcard it states, "The building was completed in 1812. Here the Southern Assembly was organized December 4, 1861. Here Woodrow Wilson worshipped throughout twelve years of his childhood, his father, the Rev. Joseph R. Wilson, D.D., served as a pastor from 1858 to 1870." Robert T. Junge writes, "Hi, Here's another picture of Augusta. The grounds of this church are beautiful. As you can see it is very old. Only a few more days. Love, Bob." Today, across from the church, the boyhood home of former U.S. president Woodrow Wilson has been restored as a museum in the heart of Augusta.

Three

The Band

The P.M.G.C. (Provost Marshal General Center) Band Room was off limits to unauthorized persons.

These soldiers are jamming during a break at a band rehearsal at a club on base known as the Barn. The soldiers playing are listed as Sammy Feenstra of California, Jim Davis of West Virginia, and Dick Klotz of Indiana. Don Benson of Illinois sits behind the band holding a baritone, while Charlie Vanatta of Indiana sits to the far right.

Gen. Edwin Parker (left) congratulates Sergeant Tarabine (right). The general enjoyed listening to the band's short concerts. Sergeant Tarabine's left arm holds a parade baton, and his arm boasts a patch that reads "Provost General."

The Provost Marshal Band is looking sharp while marching during an early morning parade outside of the barracks. The time listed is 7:40 a.m.

Here is another view of the band from the back during the 7:40 a.m. parade.

When visitors came to Camp Gordon to visit members of the band, they would often stay at motor courts such as this one in Augusta. This particular one is off of U.S. Highway 1 one mile south of the city limits.

The band is having a morning concert in front of P.M.G.C. headquarters. In the background, there is a chapel. It is of new construction, and the chapel has yet to be painted.

The band can be seen performing in front of the newly constructed chapel. Notice the pay phone next to the church.

This is Company B's graduation in August 1951. Here the future warriors perform on the parade grounds.

George Packis, Hugh Thornton, and Dick Bartlett stand together for a group photograph. The guys look sharp in their uniforms.

The band stands together in a unified four-row formation for this photograph.

This parade was conducted on a Saturday morning on October 13, 1951. It is the graduating class of Squadron M. The parade route was from the squadron area, down Fifth Avenue, to Theater No. 4. Everyone was in step!

Gen. Edwin Parker was the provost marshal general of the U.S. Army. He and Col. Jeremiah P. Holland, commandant of P.M.G.C. at Camp Gordon, watch as band members present themselves and their music to the two-person audience.

This image was taken on September 6, 1951, at Camp Gordon.

On this partly cloudy day, the boys look their best when passing in review.

In this image, the band can be seen in full form.

The band often played near the Old Post Headquarters. This monument is dedicated to the headquarters. It reads, "The Old Post Headquarters, completed 30 March 1942, is the installation's second oldest building and an excellent example of World War II architecture. Headquarters for the Fourth (Ivy) and 26th (Yankee) Infantry Division and the Tenth Armored Division resided here while the units trained for War II. At war's end, its inhabitants presided over a separation center for approximately 87,000 returning troops. Command activities continued on the site throughout both the Korean conflict and Vietnam War."

Roger Sterling relaxes before a performance.

Oftentimes the band would play for ceremonies such as the dedication of a monument. The one pictured here is dedicated to the 4th Infantry Division. The division trained at Camp Gordon from December 1941 until April 1943.

Four

BARRACK LIFE

The mess hall was always full of activity. Here two cooks take time from their busy schedule to pose for a photograph with their friends. Notice the trash can and the sign that sits above it saying "edible."

Here two military police officers step out onto a front porch for a relaxing moment in the sun. Notice the helmet being worn by the soldier.

This unidentified soldier poses for a picture to send back home to family and friends. The quote on the back of the photograph reads, "Your son—borrowed car."

A young soldier stands beneath the "Company B MP RTC Orderly Room" sign so all those at home can relate to the tremendous job he is doing of training himself to protect the United States of America.

This group photograph consists of George Parker from Ohio; Joe Ballaera from Boston, Massachusetts; Stan Okuniewski from Pennsylvania; John Lowry from Texas; Ralph Zaun from Ohio; and Sammy Feenstra (kneeling) from California.

This soldier refuses to be photographed. He may be inclined to call this photographer "early paparazzi."

Looking sharp in uniform was always a chore, but it was something that every soldier tried to perfect.

Bob Ziegler shows off his Class B winter uniform.

Joe Lobue, Luigi ?, Ralph Zaun, and Joe Ballaera (reading a book in the background) pose for a photograph outside a maintenance area.

Robert Junge poses for this photograph wearing his military police uniform.

This photograph shows the side angle of the dress uniform.

Finally, relaxation did set in with a smile for the cameraman.

Dress right! Attention! This Camp Gordon soldier stands in front of the Company B Military Police Replacement Training Center (MPRTC) orderly room for this photograph. He would make a formidable opponent in the field.

Inspection was not just a weekday event. These soldiers set formation and passed inspection early on a Saturday morning at Camp Gordon.

A group of four soldiers brave the hot sun for a photograph. Notice how tight and sharp the uniforms are in accordance with military procedure.

Sgt. Roger Sterling hangs out in his convertible while the photographer captures a candid moment. Notice the Confederate cap he is wearing.

A soldier poses outside of a World War II–era building for this photograph.

While in dress, this soldier shows that he is a no-nonsense individual when need be.

Joe Lobue, Sammy Feenstra, and Dick Koltz hang out in front of Koltz's Studebaker in a field at Camp Gordon.

Shown in this early-1950s photograph, the fire station at Camp Gordon was always on the ready. Notice the light on top of the emergency car that sits next to the fire truck. It has the classic "bubble light" situated on the top to warn vehicles and passersby of potential emergencies that fire personnel might be en route to.

This World War II–era building was burned to the ground by fire. The main appendage still standing is the brick chimney.

In this photograph, fire has ravaged several military buildings at Camp Gordon. A group of soldiers surveys the magnitude of damage done to the wooden buildings.

A lone soldier takes in the damage he sees from the fire.

The costly assessment of damage frustrates investigation teams at Camp Gordon. This frontal view of the fire damage shows how destructive the blaze really was to many buildings.

Here an angular view captures another view of the fire damage.

Troops line up in front of the mess hall. Complaints about chow have been universal in any nation's military since the dawn of organized warfare. After a hard day's routine, however, the chow still tastes quite good.

Pictured is the airfield at Camp Gordon with barracks in the background. Airplanes shown here are a Beechcraft Bonanza with the V-shaped tail, an AG Texan Military Trainer, and two Army Piper Cubs. Note the control tower.

Hanging out with the cooks was better than hanging them perhaps. Several military police trainees pose with cooks on the steps of the mess hall. Note the signs over the garbage cans. They read "non-edible trash" and "edible."

Pfc. Bob Ziegler is reading training materials that will assist him in his future military endeavors. Notice how orderly the bunks are that sit in the background. There is no rest for the weary.

Time passed inside of the barracks was often accomplished by camaraderie and conversation. Here C. H. Miller, George Packis, Joe Lobue, and an unidentified soldier have a "bull session."

Morning came early for many of the soldiers at Camp Gordon. In this image, one can see the appreciation of bunk life.

Sammy Feenstra is posing for inspection. He brings comic relief to the scene.

Two hearty cooks stand outside the mess hall of the military police training facility.

This comic show was put on by a P.M.G.C. band member for "Officer's Call." Pictured from left to right are Shanley, Tarabine, Schied, Rempe, Lanta (with bass horn), Koltz, Feenstra, and Junge.

Gen. Edwin Parker (left) celebrates a ground-breaking ceremony with Col. Jeremiah P. Holland (right) at Camp Gordon. In the background, other ranking officials look on. Colonel Holland would later be promoted to brigadier general, and he would be nominated into the U.S. Military Police Corps Hall of Fame in 2002. Another honor bestowed on Colonel Holland was an award named after him to annually honor the most outstanding military police unit.

Another view of Gen. Edwin Parker and Col. Jeremiah P. Holland at a ground-breaking ceremony at Camp Gordon is seen in this image.

The crowd listens to a speech during the ceremony.

In this image, one can see important figureheads present at the ground-breaking ceremony.

The band is prepared for a performance as top brass walks by.

Attention and perfect form are demonstrated here by the military police soldiers.

All eyes are on the speaker during this event.

In this image, a studious soldier prepares himself for the rigors of course work ahead of him. Advertisements in the background that can be seen read "The Military Police School" and "Basic Enlisted Military Police Course".

This image shows a group shot of Company B MPRTC.

Shown in this image is Company B in a group in uniform. Notice the small puppy that is being held by a soldier on the second row.

Charlie Miller smiles while Joe Edwards clowns in front of the band room.

The buildings of Casual Company are seen here. In the far right are Company E's mess hall and day room. Note the Spartan simplicity of the scene.

Casual Company's day room and mess hall are shown here. In the distance, Melvin Dickson is seen going into the day room.

In this scene, the Post Headquarters sits with astounding authority. Even so, there are only a handful of these buildings left.

The 2nd, 3rd, and 4th platoon barracks of Casual Company at Camp Gordon are shown in this photograph.

In this image, two soldiers are seen sitting in conversation. Another comes to pay a visit to see how his buddies are doing.

Soldiers think about everyday tasks as others pack their belongings for a weekend pass in nearby Augusta.

A military police officer kneels while observing the activities of other soldiers in the distance.

These unidentified soldiers are readying themselves for a practical joke by filling a riding boot with water.

In this photograph, the Signal Corps Training Center is shown as a large behemoth of a building. Here the important decisions were made by upper command. It had a simple beginning at Camp Gordon, but it now dominates Fort Gordon.

Two buildings sit next to each other on a quiet street. Notice the board next to the telephone pole that denotes base activities.

In this image, Sgt. Gordy Hardy and Sgt. Richard Pinola pose in uniform. Pinola was the sergeant for the 1st platoon.

Gen. Edwin P. Parker and Col. Jeremiah P. Holland sit thinking about the day's events. The shadow of the photographer can be seen at the bottom of the image.

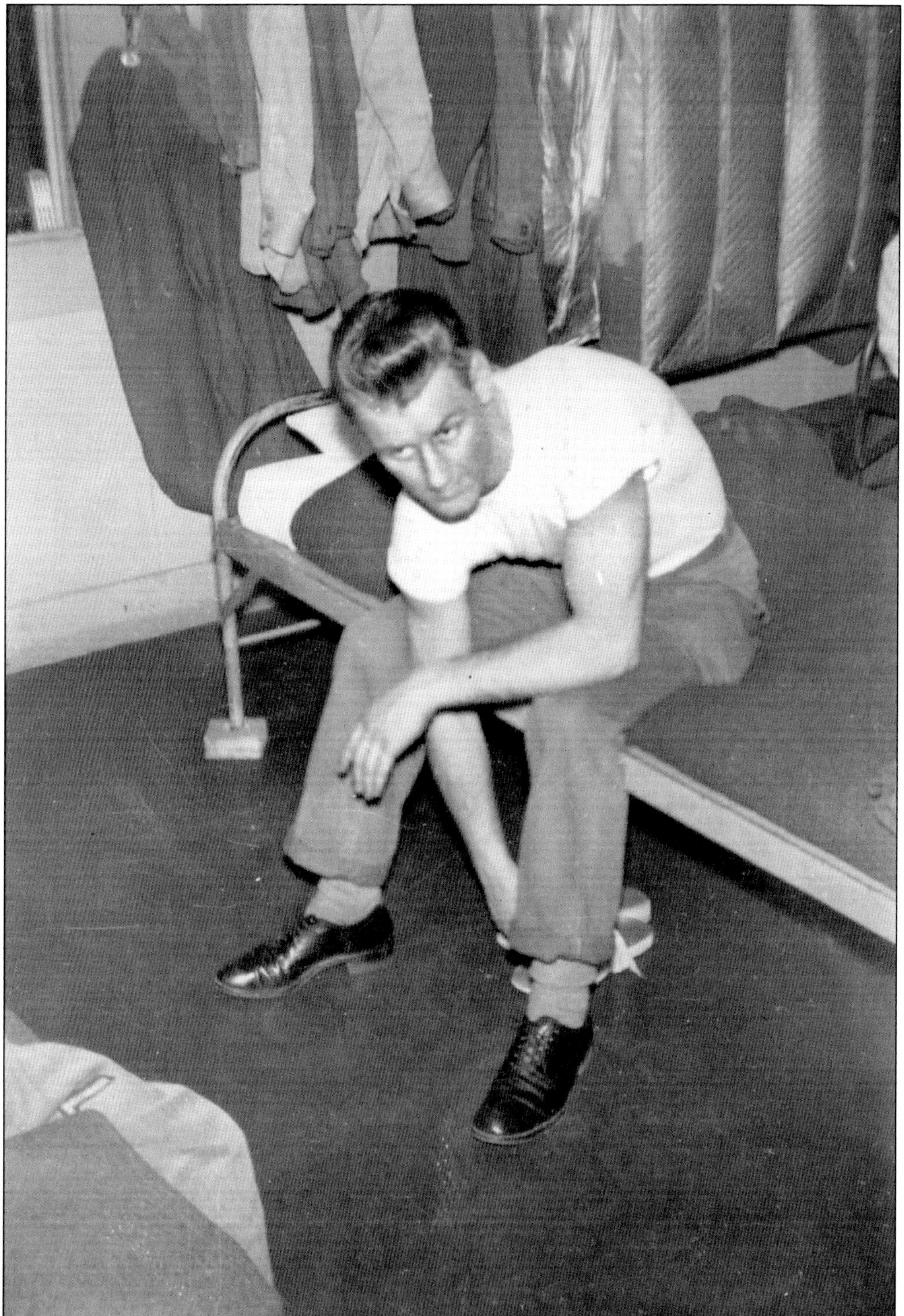

Sammy Feenstra changes shoes in this photograph. Boots, sneakers, and dress shoes were all parts of the soldier's gear.

In March 1951, these soldiers have assembled for formation. Note the waist-length "Ike" jackets in vogue during the time period. The short coat was named for Dwight David Eisenhower, supreme Allied commander in Europe in World War II. He later became the president of the United States.

Soldiers get ready for monthly pay, a most popular day. However, fines and other fees cut into the amount. Nevertheless, there'll be a hot time in the old town tonight.

“Matilda” Koltz is being sung to passionately by “Shardrack” Feenstra, accompanied by his romantic ukulele. Note the Spartan barracks.

Joe Lobue reads and relaxes. This was a time to reflect on the day's happenings and to think about family and friends back home. Note the orderliness of the room.

Four military police trainees pose beside the bus that will shortly take them to Mirror Lake at Camp Gordon for their graduation exercises from the Provost Marshal Training Course.

Everyone is on the bus readying themselves for the trip to Mirror Lake.

Five

In the Field

This group of soldiers is studying general orders before embarking on field exercises.

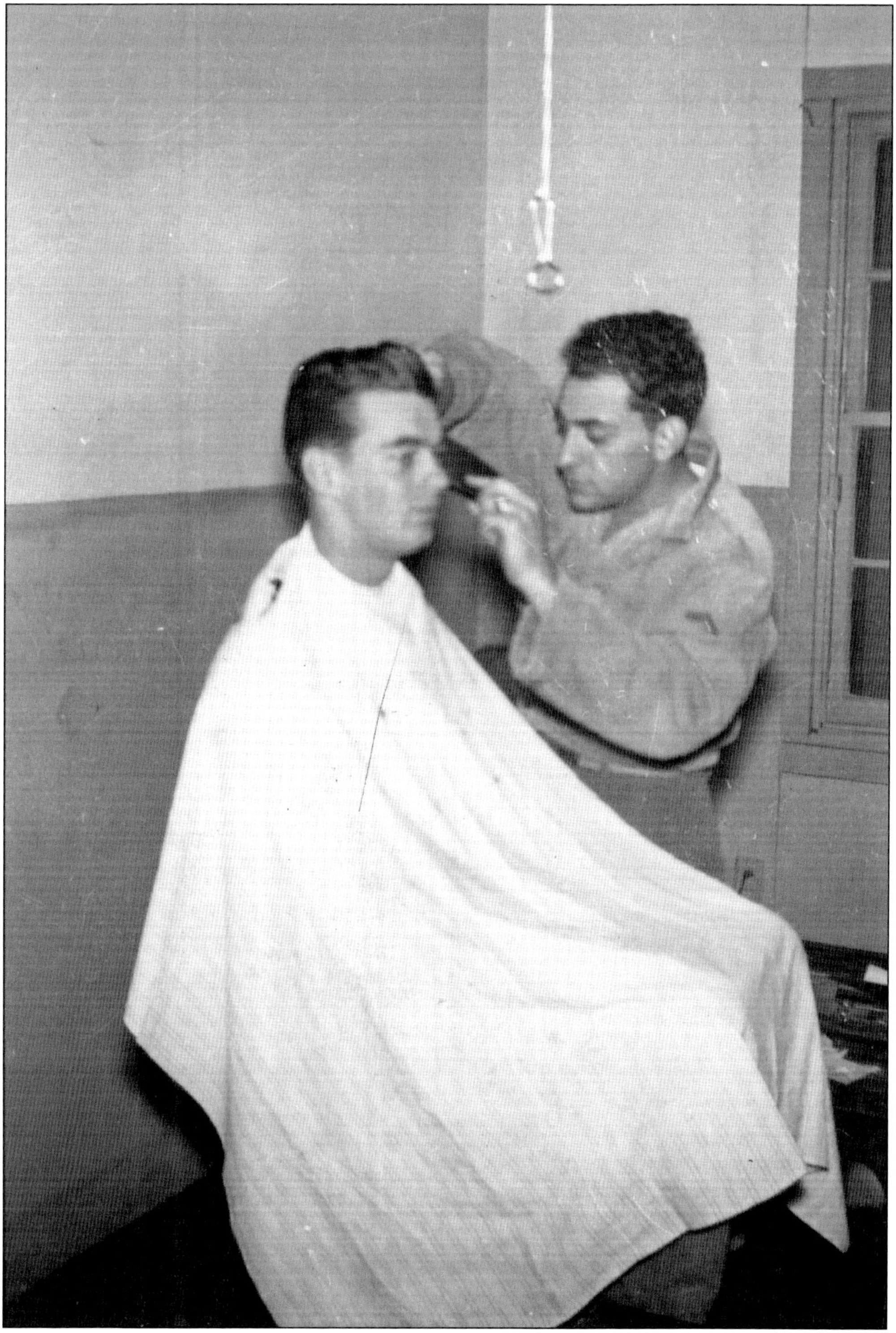

All soldiers know, like it or not, that a proper haircut has to be maintained in the military. Here Luigi ? cuts Richard Koltz's hair in his room for 50¢—the best cut in Georgia.

Here is a photograph taken from inside a vehicle on Range Road. It runs through Fort Gordon to various firing ranges. A jeep can be seen in the distance. Note the building on the left side of the road in the distance.

En route to military exercises on Range Road, a military dump truck passes by to work on a construction project.

This unidentified soldier smiles as the photographer captures a quick shot before taking off for field exercises.

Here an armored personnel carrier and its crew stop to relax and pose for the camera. Note the circular mount on top for the .50-caliber heavy machine gun.

Here is another image in front of a personnel carrier.

This group looks ready for action if they were called up for field duty.

The armored personnel carrier (APC) carried troops into combat and provided fire support. The sides are sloped to deflect incoming fire.

Charlie Vanatta, George Packis, Jim Davis, and Dick Shanley are on break at Mirror Lake.

Smiling is contagious. This soldier is enjoying a break between exercises.

In advanced infantry training (AIT), much time is spent in the classroom as well as in the field. Note the white tape on the helmets—the soldiers' last names are printed on them.

Military police were trained on all infantry weapons. Here the firing of the Model 2 Browning .50-caliber machine gun is demonstrated. A venerable weapon, its power is legendary.

Here is another view of the .50-caliber with a soldier behind the gunner holding a belt of cartridges for reloading.

Military police train with the .50-caliber heavy machine gun. Their duties often included combat situations, and they had to maintain readiness at all times.

A row of .50-caliber heavy machine guns awaits their crews on a remote firing range at Camp Gordon.

Military police trainees take five on one of Camp Gordon's rifle ranges. Note the targets in the rear.

This is an image of the .50-caliber with the receiver opened for reloading. Note the tarp-covered ammo stack in the background.

This soldier is watched over by a superior training him for combat.

The photographer "caught ya" when you least expected it.

Here is another view of firearms training. Practice makes perfect.

Here is a front view of trainees with the .50-caliber machine gun. In combat, one did not want to be where the camera is.

Two military police officers strike a truculent pose with their M1 Garands and battle gear. Their grins belie their true intentions. Much has changed in combat equipment since the early 1950s.

"Oh, my aching dogs are talking!" groaned many a trainee on long marches. Military police officers take 10 on the roadside at Camp Gordon. Note the dusty Georgia dirt road.

"Smoke 'em if ya have 'em!" was the oft-repeated command during 10-minute breaks. These soldiers are doing just that.

"Ah sleep that knits the ravell'd sleeve of care," William Shakespeare wrote. This scene shows some soldiers hard at rest after a long day of field maneuvers.

This image shows a group of soldiers before they begin field maneuvers. Notice the bayonets on the sitting soldiers.

A World War II howitzer stands guard at the Post Headquarters.

Six

Prisoners of War

Camp Gordon was a German prisoner of war camp during World War II. There is a burial ground for those who were German prisoners that died while in the southern part of the United States. The inscription on the German memorial reads, "In this burial ground rest 21 German soldiers of the Second World War."

This image shows the entire German cemetery at Fort Gordon.

Edmund Schwalbenberg held the rank of sergeant when he was taken prisoner at Viersen/Rhl. When he was captured, he had sustained injuries in North Africa. He later died at Camp Wheeler, Georgia. His tombstone reads "May 19, 1945."

Hans Salmhofer was a 23-year-old private when he was taken prisoner. He died at Camp Gordon from cancer. The Austrian's tombstone reads "November 17, 1945."

Kurt Hoessle was 26 years of age when he was taken prisoner in Africa. He was killed while on a wood-cutting detail in Charleston, South Carolina. His tombstone reads "April 30, 1945."

Wilhelm Riechmann was a 19-year-old private when he was captured in Tunisia. He was a butcher by trade. Riechmann drowned at Myrtle Beach, South Carolina, while at a prisoner of war camp. His tombstone reads "July 15, 1944."

Richard Heuther was a 23-year-old private when he was taken prisoner in Tunisia. He was an auto mechanic by trade. Heuther committed suicide as a POW in Waynesboro, Georgia. His tombstone reads "March 6, 1945."

Cpl. Friedrich Maise was 25 years of age when he was taken prisoner in Tunisia. He was a locksmith by trade. Maise passed away from an unknown injury at Florence, South Carolina. His tombstone reads "August 20, 1945."

Sgt. Heinrich Schaefstall was 31 years old when he was taken prisoner in Grenoble, France. His death was the result of an accident that occurred in Chatham, Georgia, involving a tractor and a trailer.

Karl Schroedersecker was 27 years of age when he was taken prisoner near Tivoli, Italy. Schroedersecker was a factory worker by trade. He passed away at Charleston, South Carolina. His tombstone reads "October 4, 1944."

Wilhelm Krauss was a 19-year-old private when he was taken prisoner in Remiremont, France. He was a farmer by trade. Krauss was killed in an automobile accident at Myrtle Beach, South Carolina. His tombstone reads "July 3, 1945."

Cpl. Adolf Reichert was 21 years of age when he was captured in Tunisia. He was a miller by trade. Reichert was killed when working on a pulpwood detail in Vidalia, Georgia.

Medical Cpl. Hermann Walter was 43 years of age when he was taken prisoner in Southern France. He was a compositor. Walter committed suicide at Myrtle Beach, South Carolina. His tombstone reads "May 7, 1945."

Cpl. Ludwig Janson was 24 years of age when he was taken prisoner in Tunisia. He committed suicide while being held as a POW in Waynesboro, Georgia. His tombstone reads "October 3, 1944."

Maj. Karl Heinz Werner was in Tunisia when he was taken prisoner. He was a 33-year-old physician who committed suicide at a camp in Whitemore, South Carolina. His tombstone date reads "February 4, 1946."

Sgt. Ernst Link was 23 years old when he was taken prisoner in Tunisia. He passed away from an unknown injury while incarcerated at Camp Gordon, Georgia. His tombstone reads "February 3, 1945."

Cpl. Horst Gunther was 23 years of age when he was taken prisoner in Tunisia. He was a locksmith by trade. His death was attributed to homicide while at a POW camp in Aiken, South Carolina. His tombstone reads "April 6, 1944."

Josef Lackner was 42 years of age when he was taken prisoner in France. He died from an unknown injury at Fort Jackson, South Carolina. His tombstone reads "December 2, 1944."

Erwin Kerz was taken prisoner in Tunisia in 1943. He died from a gunshot wound while at Camp Gordon. His tombstone reads "October 23, 1943."

Cpl. Christian Pfeifer was 22 years of age when he was taken prisoner in Florence, Italy. He was a painter by trade. He drowned at Cheraw State Park in South Carolina. His tombstone reads "July 13, 1945."

Cpl. Fredy Gehrmann was 24 years of age when he was taken prisoner in Africa. He had been a musician before his death, which was as a result from an accident in a lumberyard in McRae, Georgia. His tombstone reads "August 8, 1945."

Alfred Heinrich Zeller was a 19-year-old private when he was taken prisoner in Brest, France. He was a chemical worker by trade. He was killed by rope strangulation while at Camp Gordon, Georgia. His tombstone reads "November 12, 1944."

Fredrick Hamer was 44 years of age when he was taken prisoner in Aachen, Germany. He passed away from a heat stroke in Twiggs County, Georgia. His tombstone reads "August 23, 1945."

Antonio Zadel was 36 years of age and part of a construction battalion when he was taken prisoner. Not much is known of Zadel, but he died shortly after arriving at Camp Gordon. His memorial inscription reads, "In this burial ground rests an Italian soldier from the Second World War."

Even though Antonio Zadel was a POW alongside the Germans, he refused to be buried with them. The result was his body being laid to rest some 50 yards away underneath a shady canopy of trees.

Seven

History

This artifact is a pillowcase that could be purchased and sent to a relative as a souvenir from Camp Gordon. In this case, it is for someone's mother.

The U.S. Army Signal Corps Museum displays this antique license plate from Camp Gordon.

Pennants of all kinds were popular with people during the 1940s and 1950s. This is an example of one from Camp Gordon.

Shown here is a bust of Albert J. Myer on display at the U.S. Army Signal Corps Museum.

Freedom Park at Fort Gordon was designed and built on the spot where the old Post Headquarters had once stood. The park is full of dedications and monuments to those who fought for American freedom.

In this image from Freedom Park, original pieces of the Berlin wall stand as a testament to freedom after it was torn down. In regard to the wall, U.S. president Ronald Reagan stated, "Mr. Gorbachev, open this gate! Mr. Gorbachev, tear down this wall." More of the wall can be seen at the U.S. Army Signal Corps Museum at Fort Gordon.

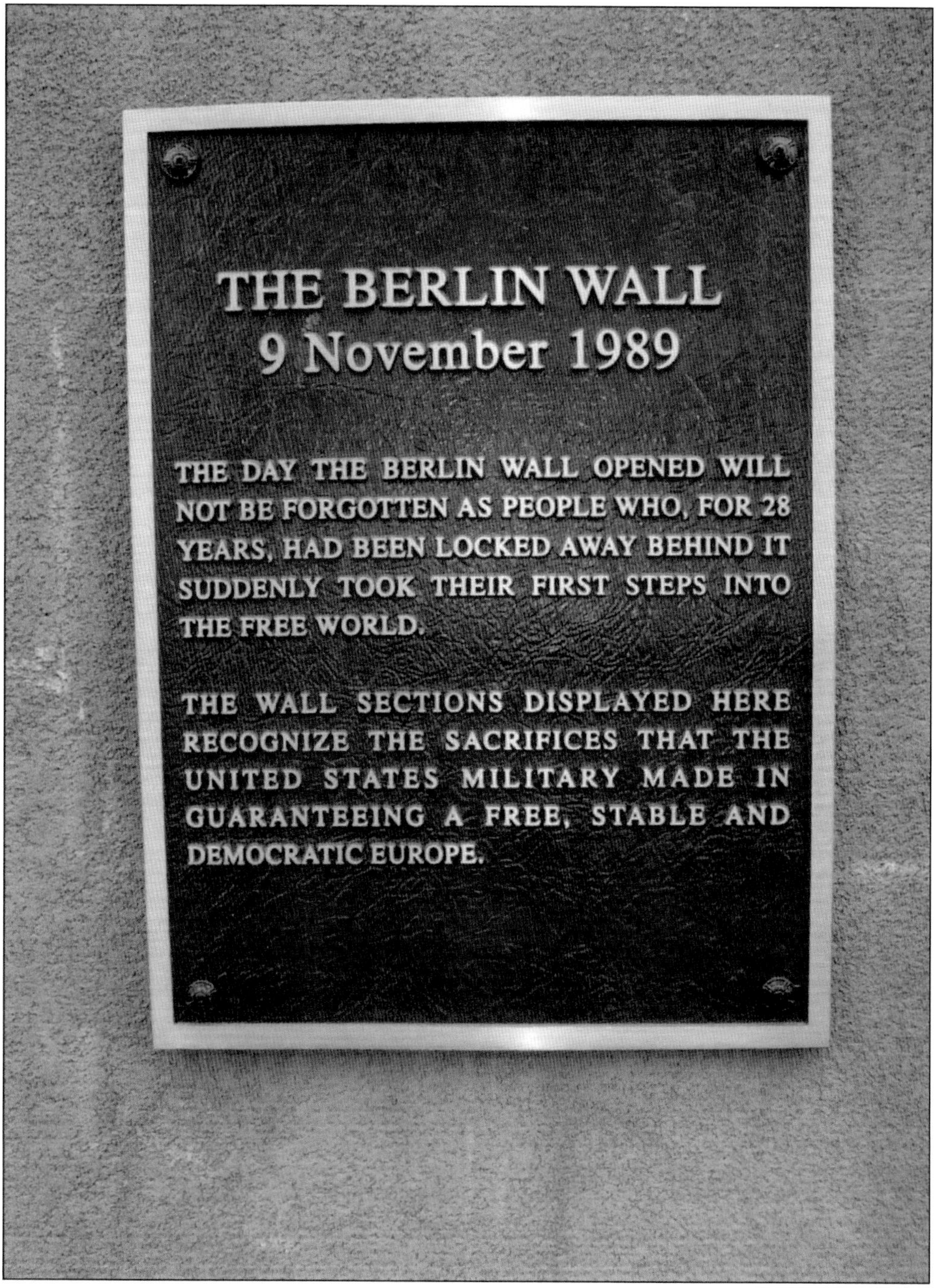

This plaque reads, "The Berlin Wall, 9 November 1989: The day the Berlin Wall opened will not be forgotten as people who, for 28 years, had been locked away behind it suddenly took their first steps into the free world. The wall sections displayed here recognize the sacrifices that the United States Military made in guaranteeing a free, stable and democratic Europe."

This monument sits on a site at Freedom Park. It is dedicated to the 10th Armored "Tiger" Division. It reads, "Dedicated to the glory of God and to the gallant men who served, trained at Camp Gordon September 1943 to August 1944."

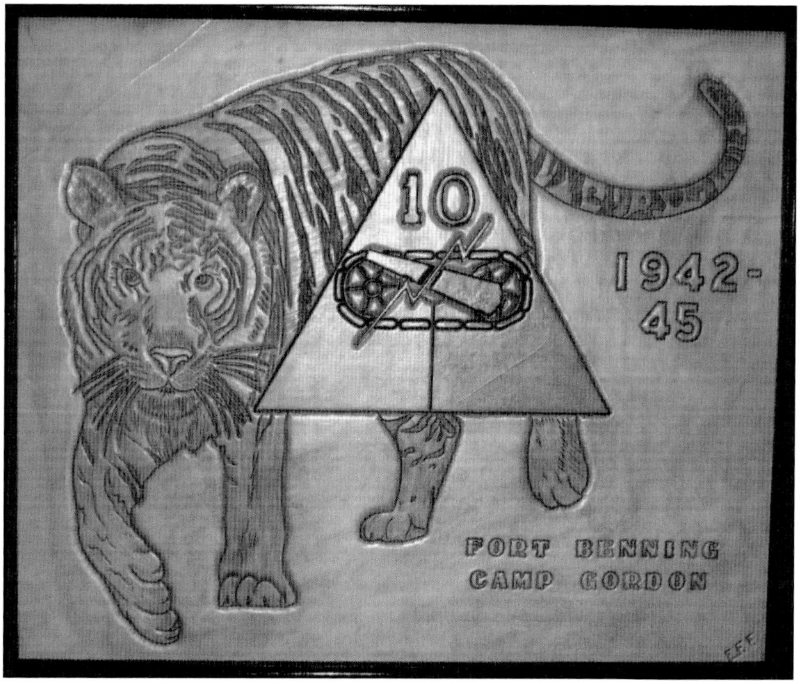

This picture of the Tiger Division hangs as an historical artifact at the U.S. Army Signal Corps Museum at Fort Gordon.

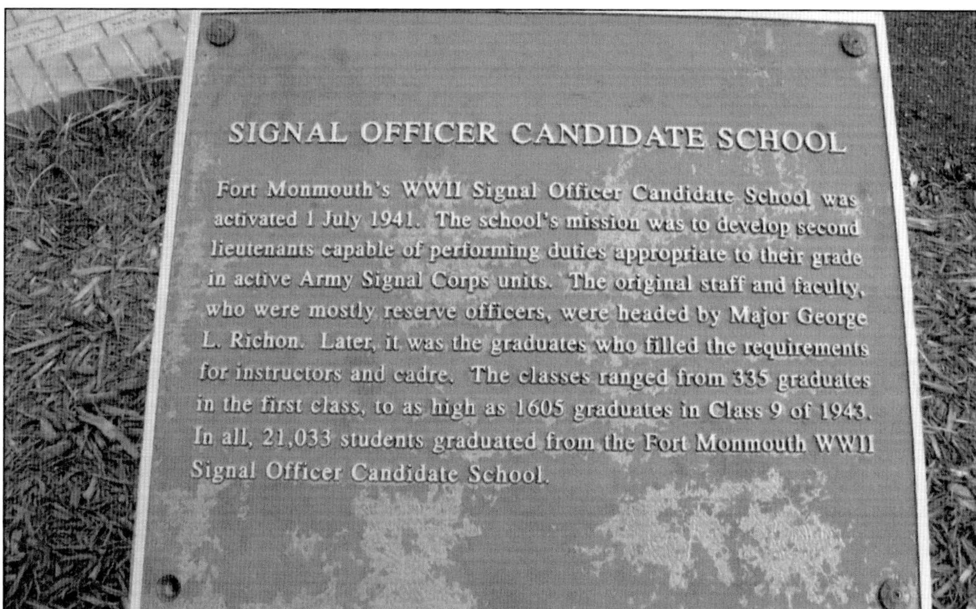

The U.S. Army Signal Corps inhabits modern-day Fort Gordon. This plaque at Freedom Park reads, "Fort Monmouth's WWII Signal Officer Candidate School was activated 1 July 1941. The school's mission was to develop second lieutenants capable of performing duties appropriate to their grade in active Army Signal corps units. The original staff and faculty, who were mostly reserve officers, were headed by Major George L. Richon. Later, it was the graduates who filled the requirements for instructors and cadre. The classes ranged from 335 graduates in the first class, to as high as 1605 graduates in Class 9 of 1943. In all, 21,033 students graduated from the Fort Monmouth WWII Signal Officer Candidate School."

The 26th Infantry Division trained at Camp Gordon from May 1943 to September 1944. This monument is dedicated to them.

The M59A1 was introduced in 1953 to replace the M75 Armored Personnel Carrier. It weighed in at 18 tons with one .50-caliber machine gun located on top. It could carry a crew of 2 plus 10 passengers.

In the 1930s, the field artillery board conducted extensive tests of the mobility of field artillery pieces. The trend was to move toward more tractor-drawn artillery. Tests were conducted with the French M-1897 75-millimeter gun, which had been widely used by the United States in World War I. To make the piece more suitable for use with motor vehicles, the carriage was modified and rubber pneumatic tires were added starting in 1936. Several other modifications were made, and the result was the designation of the modified piece as the M-2A3. The M-2A3 was primarily intended to be used by division artillery units and was pulled by a track or wheeled vehicle.

Evan Joiner stands behind the M-2A3 75-millimeter gun in this image.

The Radar Set AN/MPQ-10 entered service in 1954. It is a lightweight, transportable radar set designed to locate and track mortar and artillery shells. When used with associated recording or computer equipment, the radar set can be used to locate the point of origin and point of impact of the projectiles. The radar set consists of two major sections: the tracker mount and the radar control. The tracker mount contains radar set components mounted on a modified M2A1 40-millimeter gun carriage.

The M48 Patton Battle Tank was designed in 1953 from the M47. It carried a 90-millimeter gun and a coaxial .30-caliber machine gun mounted on the commander's cupola.

Evan Joiner is shown here standing in front of a M48 Patton Battle Tank. It is important that new generations learn of the nation's history.

This plaque is dedicated to Patrick J. Brems. It reads "Brems Barracks, dedicated in memory of Patrick J. Brems Private First Class, Military Police Corps, killed in action, Vietnam 1 April 1966."

The Kilbourne Leadership Award plaque reads, "Lieutenant Charles E. Kilbourne exemplified the leadership characteristics of the Signal Corps officer. He was awarded the Medal of Honor on 6 May 1905 for his dedication to duty at Paco Bridge during the Philippine Insurrection, 1899. His citation reads: 'Within a range of 250 yards of the enemy and in the face of rapid fire, (he) climbed a pole at the east end of the bridge and, in the full view of the enemy, coolly and carefully repaired a broken telegraph wire, thereby reestablishing communication to the front.' The Kilbourne award is presented to the one student of each class who demonstrates the most leadership potential during the conduct of the course."

Discover Thousands of Local History Books Featuring Millions of Vintage Images

Arcadia Publishing, the leading local history publisher in the United States, is committed to making history accessible and meaningful through publishing books that celebrate and preserve the heritage of America's people and places.

Find more books like this at
www.arcadiapublishing.com

Search for your hometown history, your old stomping grounds, and even your favorite sports team.

Consistent with our mission to preserve history on a local level, this book was printed in South Carolina on American-made paper and manufactured entirely in the United States. Products carrying the accredited Forest Stewardship Council (FSC) label are printed on 100 percent FSC-certified paper.

MADE IN THE USA